THE WINNING CV BLUEPRINT

THE GUIDE FOR WRITING ATTENTION GRABBING CVs EVEN IF YOU ARE A RECENT GRADUATE WITH NO WORK EXPERIENCE.

The Winning CV Blueprint

The Winning CV Blueprint

Copyright © 2018 Ebenezer Anifowose.

ISBN: 9781983113581

All rights reserved. No part of this publication must be reproduced whether in full or in part without the written express approval from the publishers.

Disclaimer: The information in this book/eBook is provided for educational purposes to guide you to write winning CVs that can get an employer's attention. While the information in this book/eBook will prove very vital and helpful, the author or publishers provides no guarantees that you will get any result as getting the results you seek will be solely based on your level of effort and persistence.

Independently Published:
Ebenny Innovative Consults (Ebenny Inc.)
P.O.Box 125, Sango Ota
Ogun State, Nigeria.
ebennyinc@yahoo.com

The Winning CV Blueprint

CONTENTS

CHAPTER ONE 7
THE WINNING CV MINDSET 7
    Introduction 7
    Why do you write a CV? 8
    Difference between a CV and a Résumé 9
    Your CV is your first impression 9
    Think like the employer 11
    Your first job 13
    Who is more frustrated? 14
CHAPTER TWO 16
THE WINNINIG CV ARCHITECTURE 16
    Introduction 16
    The Heading 16
    Bio-data 16
    Career Profile or Statement 21
    Education & Qualification 24
    Work Experience/ Employment History 26
    Skills 28
    Other Sections 29
    References 30
    Layout and Format 33

CHAPTER THREE	36
THE WINNING CV DYNAMICS	36
What is a Dynamic CV	36
Steps to Write a Dynamic CV	39
CHAPTER FOUR	44
FINE POINTS OF THE WINNING CV	44
Types of CVs	44
Recent Graduate with Little or No Experience	45
Changing Careers	46
Dealing With Gaps in Your Career	47
Getting Your Winning CV to Recruiters	48
Understanding Applicant Tracking Systems	51
APPENDICES	53
Appendix 1 – Standard CV Sample	53
Appendix 2 – Skill Based CV Sample	55
Appendix 3 – Career Specific CV Types	57
Technical CV	57
Creative industries CV	57
Video CV	57
Academic CV	58

PREFACE

Writing winning CVs is mostly a frame of mind and this is why I have written this book. Firstly, to open your mindset to think like employers and secondly, to help you reflect and communicate in writing so you can help employers achieve their objectives of filling a new role easily.

This book is a practical hands-on resource that can guide you to write an excellent CV from scratch. The first chapter dwells on the winning CV mindset while chapter two breaks down the structure of a winning CV. Chapter three to discuss Dynamic CVs, a very important part of a winning CV that will land you your dream job.

In chapter four, you will learn about other important things to know on CVs which includes how to position yourself whether you are a fresh graduate, changing careers or having gaps in your employment history. You will also learn about the formats to save your CV in and how to compose emails for job applications.

I hope you enjoy this book as much as I have enjoyed reading it

So Far, So God.
Ebenezer Anifowose

CHAPTER ONE

THE WINNING CV MINDSET

Introduction
It will be logical to start this chapter by defining a CV and providing a detailed explanation of what it means, but I will rather start with the end in mind- the actual reason you are reading this book I suppose.

What is a 'Winning CV'?

I will tell you with no beating around the bush. A winning CV is that CV that gets you shortlisted, invited for an interview or contacted for follow up discussion. Beyond that, a winning CV also gets you the job, other things being equal.

There are many reasons why you might not be shortlisted or get an interview invitation, however, it should not be because of the fact that you have a poor CV; a CV that cannot convince the recruiter that you truly qualify for the job.

For every of your job applications where you are asked to submit a CV, your mindset should be that you either submit a winning CV or do not bother to apply at all.

This mindset helps you put in all the hardwork required to churn out a winning CV for every of your job applications.

Are you ready for the mindset shift that helps you achieve this?

I can hear you scream Yes! That is why you have this book in your hands in the first place.

Now that we are on the same page, let's move on, shall we?

What is a CV?

CV is actually an acronym for the Latin word 'Curriculum Vitae' which means "course of life". In essence a CV is a document which tells a story of your course of life that the employer will be interested in.

Why do you write a CV?
This is probably a dumb question. Isn't it? Everyone knows we write one when applying for jobs.

That's right. Actually, CVs are not only for job applications. Students or scholars who are applying for admission into certain programs also submit CVs. They are also required by some corporate bodies to process loan or grant applications. While there are many CV formats with no particularly best format, the purpose of writing the CV and the expected requirements will logically determine the structure of the CV.

Now let me ask a more sensible question. You apply for a job because you want to get selected or win, why then, would you not put in your best? Yes! You would. There's absolutely no reason and I know that is why you are reading this now.

Difference between a CV and a Résumé

Before I continue, it will be important to clarify the difference between a Résumé and Curriculum Vitae.

While curriculum vitae is the Latin for "course of life", In contrast, Résumé is the French word for "summary." Both of them are documents tailored to a specific job or company you are applying to. They are both used to get you an interview and should represent you as the best qualified candidate.

See Table A highlighting the differences between a CV and a Résumé

Your CV is your first impression

A CV is a document showing the details of your relevant skills, experience and achievements. Take note of the word, "relevant". You do not have to list everything you know or every experience you have. But you have to identify the most relevant information that would interest the employer.

Some people are of the opinion that they have to be modest about their CV. Being modest is not a virtue in this case. You have to learn to market yourself as best as you can.

The Winning CV Blueprint

Differences between a Résumé and a CV

	Résumé	CV
Meaning	French origin meaning "summary"	Latin origin meaning "course of life"
Contents	Lists education and work history, experiences and a brief summary of skills.	A more detailed explanation of education, work experience and skills including achievements awards and honours
Length	Shorter (1 page)	Longer, and can be of varying length (2-10 pages) long.
Employer preference	Usually requested for in the US	Usually requested for in the UK and some EU countries

Table A

The employer does not know all of the applicants, all they probably have is the hundreds of CV from which they have to make a shortlist. Your CV is your marketing tool. It is your trumpet and you better blow it because if you don't, no one else will?

Your CV is the only way your employers get to 'meet' you and with which they form their first impression of you. It is important then that you create a good first impression. Your CV needs to create the correct picture of you that fits into the employer's needs. A winning CV must keep the interest of an employer and make them want to have a conversation (interview) with you.

Think like the employer
I will mention 3 major scenarios out of many that require you to send in your CV for job applications.

1. You are applying for a specific job for which you have been asked to submit a CV with or without a cover letter. This is the most common scenario where you are responding to a job advert.

2. You are uploading your CV to a job website. Here, you upload your CV to a job website specifying the sector you are specialized in so when employers visit such websites, your CV can come up in a search.

3. You are sending out CVs and letters to prospective employers even though they have not requested for applications for any role. This is you basically prospecting by sending your CV to people you think might have a job offer for you or can link you up to someone who does.

In any of the three cases above, you will always need to think like the employer or prospective employer if you would write a winning CV and capture the employer's attention.

To drive home the point of why you need to think like the employer while drafting your CV, consider the scenario below.

Four years from now, you run your own company with over 30 staff members in your head office only and you have branches in 5 countries across 2 continents.

You are expanding and you need to fill a vacancy quickly. You put out the adverts and in three days, you get about 500 CVs in response to the advertised role which needs just one person. You could have contracted it out to a recruiting agency but because the role is very important and you trust your guts, you wanted to handpick the person yourself.

You know there is likely a handful of qualified and well experienced people who have applied but the challenge is, you have 500 CVs to sift through to find this 'special one' Meanwhile, you are busy with some other business tasks which require your ongoing attention so you are under some pressure to meet all your targets.

When you eventually get the chance to go through the 500 CVs in order to shortlist 5 who would be invited for the interview, what will you be looking for?

Will you look twice at a CV that looks illegible, unreadable or distracting from the first page? Will you continue to read any that has spelling errors in the first few lines? Would you bother to flip to the second page of a CV that is scanty and looks like that of someone with no more than one year experience when you are trying to recruit for a role requiring a minimum of 3 years' experience?

I am guessing you will answer 'No' for all the questions.

The Winning CV Blueprint

Your first job

Dear Applicant. There is a job you have to do before you get the job you want and it is a simple job. The first job that determines whether you get the actual job is simple. It is to make it easy for the employer to match your experience and skills to the specific needs of the role they are recruiting for.

The easier you make this for the employer, the higher your chances of getting an invitation to an interview. Note that you might be well qualified for a job but the employer finds it difficult to see that you are the person they need. A winning CV is one which makes the employer nod and smile when reading it because of the joy of identifying one of the best candidates for the job. How do you make it easy for the employer you might ask? You make it easy by blowing your trumpet to the music beat of the employer.

To shortlist CVs, professional recruiters and HR executives will use a checklist to match potential employee's application against the skill and person requirements for the job, just like they do in interviews. This is the standard and only way they can objectively evaluate each candidate and shortlist based on the highest scores and other criteria that has been set. See this checklist as the marking scheme.

You also need to bear in mind that it might not be only the HR that will read through your CV, your soon-to-be line manager or the general manager might also read it and any or all of them can be responsible for the final shortlist.

The Winning CV Blueprint

Who is more frustrated? The applicant or the recruiter

While you are frustrated and whining about not getting any feedback from employers after sending tons of CV applications, the recruiters and employers are also frustrated about not finding a suitable candidate to fill in the vacant position after spending lots of money, time and energy.

Employers are always very careful about the recruitment process much more than you think. Have you considered how much money the company loses each day that the position remains vacant and there is no one to do the job? Can you imagine the stress the company and other staff members go through to cover up for having one less staff than they need?

Have you considered how much it cost the company to advertise in a newspaper or in a credible job website where they have the higher chance of getting in front of very qualified and experienced professionals that they seek? Do you know that the recruiter has to pend other important tasks to spend days and probably weeks to read through hundreds if not thousands of CVs just to fill one vacant position?

If the employer outsources the recruitment to an HR firm, just because they wouldn't have the time to do it themselves, do you know how much they will have to pay the recruitment firm just to fill in one position? Do you know some HR firms collect a percentage of the net salary of each employee they recruit for the employer as their consultancy fees?

Imagine the frustration, if at the end of the day after investing lots of resources in the hiring process, the employer is not convinced that they have seen the ideal candidate. They are back to square one and the longer the position remains vacant, the more stress the company goes through and the more losses they make.

I said it earlier and I will say it again. Your 'first job that determines whether you get the actual job' is simple. Make it easy for the employer to see you as the perfect candidate to fill the vacant role.

You can do this effectively by appropriately highlighting your experience and skills to match the specific needs the employer wants. You need to put forward your relevant skills, experience and achievements in a way that checks off with the person and job requirement needed for the position and make it easy for HR see. Don't write anything that will require them to read in between the lines. Do not leave any room for assumptions or guesses.

From here, we move on to chapter two which discusses the winning CV architecture. In the next chapter, you will learn the elements of a good CV, the irrelevant information to remove from a CV and how to achieve a good CV structure, form and content.

CHAPTER TWO

THE WINNING CV ARCHITECTURE

Introduction
In the previous chapter, we talked about cultivating the right mental attitude to write a winning CV and the mental acumen to think like the employer. In this second chapter, we will go on to consider the architecture and layout of a winning CV.

Whether you want to write a winning CV from scratch or you want to edit your current CV to become a winning CV, you will need to understand the winning CV architecture or structure. I will like to reiterate that there is no best CV format, but in this chapter you will get a good understanding of the elements of a winning CV which would ensure your CV has all the winning elements and does not include the elements of a losing CV.

Let's delve right in.

The Heading
There is absolutely no need to add a heading such as 'Curriculum Vitae' or 'Résumé' at the top of your CV.

Bio-data
Name & Contact Details: Present your name and contact details at the top of the CV. Your name should be bold and legible sitting right at the top of the CV. For the order of the

names, I will recommend using the standard name format which is as follows:

First Middle and Last Names

>i.e.*Ebenezer Opeyemi Anifowose.*

If you chose to use just two names, that will of course be your

First Name & Last Name.

>i.e.*Ebenezer Anifowose*

You can also use a reverse order of your name i.e.

Last Name, First Name and Middle (for three names)

Last Name & First Name (for two names)

Can you use four names? What exactly would that achieve if you do?

If you have a very long first name, it is not entirely wrong to shorten your first name on a CV but be aware that more often than not, the employer will identify you with your first name throughout the interview process and eventually when you get the job.

The other thing to be aware of is to ensure you use the name that you have on your certificates. Some people have lost job opportunities after scaling through the application process only for HR to find out that the name the applicant used to apply is different from the name on the certificates.

For your contact details, the most important are the following:

A functional phone number: This is a no brainer. Include your best mobile number on which you can be reached 24 hours every single day of the week. It is advisable you include two numbers just in case anything happens to your major line. If you do not have another line, you can include the mobile of your siblings, spouse, parents or best friend. Do well to inform the person that you used their phone numbers in your CV. That way, they are mentally expecting a call or SMS from an employer on your behalf so they do not hang up the phone or delete that important interview invitation text message.

A traceable physical address: This is straight forward. Some employers before they select the best candidate for some sensitive roles will do a spot check on your address or send your letter via courier. You should not miss any job because they could not locate your address. If the employer asks for a correspondence address, do include a postal address if you have one as they can also send communication via post.

Lastly, some jobs are location specific and the employer specifies that only residents of a city and environs should apply. Don't join those who frustrate employers who have specified clearly that candidates who do not live in ABC need not apply. Don't join the hundreds of people who live in XYZ miles apart and go ahead to apply adding more 'waste' papers to the recruiter's desk or email inbox.

If you really want the job and do not mind moving to the new location, it will then be wise to use the address of a family member or trusted friend who stays in that city in your CV and application so you increase your chances of getting the

The Winning CV Blueprint

job. You can do this because you have an intention to relocate if you get the job.

I will like to mention however that some organizations, mostly big organizations and international corporations do not care about the location of the prospective employee, especially for mid to senior level executive roles as they are willing to pay for the cost of travel to attend the interview and the cost of relocation if they eventually employ someone who stays in another state or country.Such organizations are concerned about getting the best hands for the job no irrespective of your current location.

When you apply to such firms, you can use your home address even if the job is in another state. When they want to cover transportation to attend interviews, they pay for travel from the address (state) on your CV to the address (state) of the interview usually the Headquarters of the firm.

A functional and easily accessible email: Ensure your email is formal and presentable and the best way to do this is to use your name combination i.e. 'ebenani', 'ebenezer.anifowose', 'e.anifowose'. If you cannot secure any combination of your name as an email address, you can use any other very presentable email.

You want to be sure that you use an email that you have access to 24 hours a day as you do not miss any email from the employer. Ensure you sync your email and set up notifications on your phone. Many people have lost job opportunities because they only got to read the interview invitation after the date had passed. If you still have limited access to the internet, and you are actively submitting job applications, I recommend that you check your emails for messages at least three times a day; in the morning at mid-day and in the evening just before you go to bed.

Date of Birth: This information is particularly optional and not at all important. Sometimes it can be a disadvantage to have it on the CV because of age discrimination. However, if the job has a maximum age requirement, you can add it to remove all benefit of doubt especially if you have a very impressive CV. In any case, if the employer is really impressed with your CV, they will likely want to have a discussion with you in an interview before making conclusions.

State of Origin and Local Government Area: Why will any employer need this information? Or do you think your state of origin on your CV can give you favours? Well except it is a local government specific job for indigenes. On the contrary, having such information on a CV can be a great disadvantage and it can be a basis for discrimination? What recruiters want is someone who can perform excellently on the job and unless your CV is convincing enough, having unnecessary details such as these is a complete waste of space.

Nationality: Unless you are applying for a job in another country other than the one you live in, leave out your nationality from your CV. It is just pointless to add this information.

Gender: This is another detail that is not essential on a CV, especially if your name is sex specific. It's also best to leave it out of a CV to avoid discrimination. However, if the employer specified the preferred sex they need to fill the vacant position and your name is not sex specific, do go ahead to include this detail on your CV.

Marital Status: This information does not add to the strength of your application and is not needed by the employer. Having it in your CV when the employer has not specifically requested for it can be a disadvantage creating more focal points for some form of discrimination.

Career Profile or Statement
The career profile is sometimes used interchangeably with professional profile or summary. There is a slight difference between these terms but they invariably mean the same thing. The major differences will be between a Personal and Career Profile. Personal profile focuses on the applicant's strengths and skills while Career profile includes the career goals and aspirations.

Generally, the information you want to present here is the blurb of your career, a very short overview of your skills, experience, expertise and career goals or interests. Recent graduates are more likely to use personal profiles to share their skills and ambitions while more mature professionals who have developed expertise in a field might use a career profile to outline their specific experience and expertise and their career goals for the future.

This section is optional but if well written proves to be a very important part of your CV. Research suggests that recruiters spend 8.8 seconds on a CV to decide whether they want to continue reading the CV for another 20 seconds. A short profile gives them a good reason to want to read on. However, it is best you do not include this section if you would not be able to put in a convincing profile.

You will need to be very specific and not put in a generalized profile that does not speak to the job or career you are applying for. You should not use a generic statement or copy verbatim from someone else's personal statement. A generic statement is one that anyone can use verbatim (without a need to change anything) successfully on their CV.

For application submitted through online career sites that use algorithms and bots to screen applications at the first stage, a CV with generic statements that contains no important keywords relevant to the job would not pass the screening test as the bot would not pick them up when it swipes through the database.

If you are not writing something that shows your personal voice, it is better not to write this section at all. Generic skills that anyone can have such as writing, teamwork, problem solving skills does not look good on a CV when they are not backed up with proofs. Some of these generic skills might not even be relevant to the job being applied for. It is better not to write anything at all here than to annoy the recruiter before getting the chance to see your experience.

You should use your professional profile to convince the employer that they need to pay attention and read your CV more carefully to the end.

The Winning CV Blueprint

See two examples below of a well written and a badly written personal profile.

OLUWAJACOB ABRAHAM

Location: 38, Welfare Quarters, Fiditi, Oyo Stat
Telephone: 08012345678
Email: o.abraham@gmail.com

Professional profile

To rise to the peak of my career as a public health specialist in the developmental sector taking up strategic roles and driven with a passion to increase the access of the most vulnerable to appropriate and quality healthcare locally and globally.

Sample A.

OLUWAJACOB ABRAHAM

Location: 38, Welfare Quarters, Fiditi, Oyo Stat
Telephone: 08012345678
Email: o.abraham@gmail.com

Professional profile

I am a vibrant, energetic, diligent, brilliant and goal-oriented graduate ready to contribute to achieve the objectives of any organization.

Sample B.

Can you spot the difference? Which has a generic profile and which will form part of a winning CV?

Other good examples are:
- *I am looking for a challenging, fast-paced environment within the transport and supply chain industry to utilize my acquired knowledge and develop my problem solving skill-set further.*
- *I am looking to re-establish a career in a progressive organization which requires engineering expertise, after a short career break to take care of a new-born.*

Education & Qualification

Your educational history with the qualifications obtained would usually come next after your 'career profile' but this depends on the kind of CV you are writing i.e. skills based CV or experience based CV. If you already have a lot of work experience in your industry, you can present your experience instead and then your education and qualification at a later section in your CV.

Some CV formats separate Education from Qualification and presents these in two separate sections. In my opinion, this is an unnecessary repetition. It would be pointless trying to first list out the schools attended before talking about the qualifications you got from the schools in another section. If for every education you had, you earned a qualification, it is therefore logical to have them both presented in the same section on the CV. It saves space and makes your CV tell a coherent story.

Your Grades: If you finished with a second class lower or a third class, there is absolutely no need to add the class of your grade to your CV. This is common sense. You do not want to include unnecessary information in your CV that is not screaming 'employ me immediately'. You might have had a poor grade due to many reasons but putting it on a CV when you have not been asked to can be focal point for discrimination especially when there is competition.

However, if you had a first class, you can include it. You have every reason to shout about that. If the employer requests for a particular grade class for the job and you meet up with the requirement, there is no need stating the obvious. Even if you do not meet the criteria and you want to make an attempt, then that is more reason not to include your grade on your CV.

I have said it before and would reiterate it. If you are only making an attempt at a job that you do not meet all the requirements, ensure you are putting in a very good and classic application. Do not waste the time of the employer by increasing the number of CVs of unqualified people that they have to go through.

Chronology: When listing your qualification, always start with the most recent education you obtained and then the one before that one. Note that you do not necessarily have to include all the qualification you have obtained in your life if they are in no way relevant to the job.

When I say 'in no way relevant', you have to be sure this is the case because a very vital part of writing a winning CV is finding the relevancies in seeming irrelevancies.

Gong as far back as college (secondary school) is about enough. There is absolutely no need to mention your primary school education except that is your highest qualification. Add the start and finish dates (year especially) and If you know the months of admission and graduation for each qualification, you can add them provided it wouldn't cause incoherence on your CV.

Work Experience/ Employment History

The Winning CV Blueprint

The first thing you should know is that, you do not have to include all the work experience you have had in your lifetime in every CV you submit. If there is any work experience that is not at all relevant to the job you are one you are applying for.

Chronology: When listing your experience, start with the most recent 'relevant' work experience. Then list the one before that and on you go down the list. Remember to include the time period spent on each job you listed. Include the months if you know them but ensure there is no conflict on the chronology of your work experience. It is fine to have gaps in between the jobs you have had, but be ready to explain the reason for the gaps at the interview when you are shortlisted.

Remember, that while you do not have to list the irrelevant work experiences that can distract the recruiter, you have to be sure you are excluding a truly irrelevant work experience. This is because as I said earlier, the way to truly write a winning CV is to find the relevancies in seeming irrelevant past roles.

Some CV formats have the dates on the right while others have it on the left. Wherever, you choose to put it, ensure it stands out and is easy to read.

Job Role/ Responsibilities: For every work experience you list on your CV, it is vital you include your job roles or responsibilities.

So how do you write your job roles? You simply list out the key responsibilities you had on the job. This would include your deliverables and day to day task which can be mostly backed up by your job description. Although there are times when you take up roles which are not stated on your employment letter

To write the job role for a past work experience, as much as possible, always start the sentence with an action word or verb in the past tense. These action words are also called Power Words. See example C below with the power words highlighted.

> Nov 2014–Oct 2015 **Classroom Manager**
> Community Secondary School, Obrikom, Rivers
> Responsibilities:
> - Facilitated learning by leading discussions, asking open-ended questions and enabling active participation of student.
> - Managed a classroom of over 50 students.
> - Monitored and evaluated students' performance by providing one - on- one support.

Sample C.

However, if you want to write job roles for a position you currently hold, you could use the continuous tense or any other appropriate tense of the verb.

Key Achievements: Immediately after your job responsibilities, you should highlight the key achievements you had on the job. A fresh graduate or anyone with between one to two years' experience can probably get away with not including key achievements. However, as your progress and acquire more substantial work experience, you should list your key achievements to make your CV stand out. Key achievements help employers see at a glance the kind of success you have recorded in the past. The logic is simple; if you did it before, you can do it again. It is assumed that with the right motivation and working environment, the potential candidate can achieve much more on the new job.

Voluntary Work/ Projects: It might be helpful if you can split up your work experience into Relevant Experience and use another heading such as "Additional Experience", "Other Work Experience", which can also include your voluntary work experiences, Industrial placements, student jobs and internships especially if they were not a paid role. However, this does not mean you need to write IT, SIWES in front of the jobs or describe them as such.

Whether it was a student job or placement, the organization has a name, you performed some roles and the role has a job title. Use these accordingly on your CV. If you were not officially given a title, it is completely okay to use the equivalent of the role you performed on your CV. What I am trying to say is, if you were simply called IT student at the firm but you were supporting the laboratory scientist with all laboratory work. It is completely fine to write Assistant Laboratory Officer on your CV because if you were to be a full time staff there, you would have probably carried that title.

Skills

This section is very important and is your chance to show the employer that you have a wide range of skills required for the job. Depending on the skill requirement for the job you are applying for, you will need to clearly highlight the skills you have that matches those sought by the employer. It will also be very helpful if you do not only list the skills but mention how and where you developed them or put them to use.

There are largely two types of skills and you can highlight any of them which has a potential on your CV

Transferable skills: They are not discipline specific and can be learnt in one setting and applied in another job setting or role. They can also be learnt from informal settings, volunteering, hobbies or formal work experiences. Examples include communication, teamwork, problem solving and leadership.

Knowledge skills: Are discipline specific and shows your level of expertise. You can acquire these from experience, training or academics. Examples include laboratory work, technical skills, field work and so on.

Other Sections
Honours, Awards
This is optional. If you have any achievements and awards or if you have received any form of recognition, you can list them here. Ensure you give enough information that can help readers understand the context of the award. As a minimum, include the title of the award you received, the award body's name and the date of the award.

If you are not a recent graduate, it is better off mentioning honours that you received in a work environment. Dwelling too much on award from secondary school and university might suggest you do not have any award in the most recent years.

Trainings, Membership, Certifications
This section is optional but vital if you have key certifications and trainings that are relevant to the job. You should also

always list the most relevant ones in a chronological order with the most recent at the top of the list.

Conferences, Publications, Seminars
Academic CVs for scholars and teaching at tertiary level have more need for this section of a CV. There is no way one will be a lecturer without having a number of seminars, publications and conferences attended under the hat. If you need to add this section, present all of the relevant trainings, conferences and publications based on the purpose of the CV you are writing

Hobbies and Interests: This section provides a great opportunity to illustrate your personality and let the employer get to meet you if you both ignore the fact that you are seeking employment for a few seconds. However, if all you can say is reading and travelling, it is probably best you do not include a hobbies section. What are you reading? Where are you travelling to?

References
References are usually required by employers and if you do have sufficient space on your CV, you can include at least two referees. While most organization will contact your references after an offer has been made, some organization's policy requires that references are contacted before a candidate is invited for interview and you will likely be informed about this on the job advert granting consent to have your references contacted before an offer is given.

Some candidate assume that employers consider the referee section of the CV to shortlist applicants for interviews. Would you invite someone to an interview just because the person used a popular medical doctor in your city, knows the local government chairman or a senator as a referee? I do not think so.

Most employers will not bother to contact referees until after an interview and after they have decided to give you an offer of employment. More often than not, you will likely be asked to fill out a referee form before or after the interview. It is usually this list that the employer reckons with.

If you are battling with keeping your CV short and under two pages, you can do without a referee section and simply add a line "References can be provided on request". If you have enough space, then go ahead and add references. And if you will supply references, include the full name, phone number and email contact.

Relatives are usually not to be used as referees except specifically instructed to provide such. Be aware that there are basically two types of references as seen below.

Academic Reference: This is a referee who knows you from the academic setting. Usually, this will be a lecturer in your school if not your project supervisor or departmental and faculty lecturers.

Character reference: This is someone who knows you personally from any other setting apart from work. This person should be able to vouch for your character and person.

Professional/ Employment Reference: A professional reference is someone who has worked with you in any capacity either as an employer, superior, colleague or subordinate. They usually provide reference regarding your work ethic and expertise.

If the type of reference required is not specified, you can provide one referee from each category or provide three employment references if you have had very significant work experiences.

Do not forget to inform your references that you will be using them as references on your job applications from time to time. It will not be a good ending if the reference you have supplied cannot give any positive recommendation about you because they cannot even remember who goes by your name. In addition, let them know the kind of jobs you are applying to so that they can know how best to recommend you when asked for it.

Now let us go on to discuss layout and formatting. This is another aspect of a winning CV.

Layout and Format
There is no single format for a good CV and formatting preferences will vary from country to county. The general quality a CV has to possess is that it should be legible and easy to read even when scheming through.

One way to quickly evaluate the quality of a CV is to hold it at arm's length in front of you with one hand and see if you appreciate the layout at that distance.

The Winning CV Blueprint

Paper Size and Type: The generally accepted paper type for CVs is clear white, good quality A4 paper (80-120g). The same one generally used in basic printers. It would be inappropriate to use anything smaller or bigger. If you are in the creative industry i.e. fine, graphic, creative and theatre arts you can show your ingenuity by doing unconventional things with your CV. i.e. i.e. use another paper size, opt for another paper colour. Small leaps like this have the potential to stand you out from the competition. Be careful not to overdo this.

Font Type and Size: It is best to stick to legible fonts such as Arial, Calibri, Georgia, Tahoma or Verdana which are all modern fonts easy on the eyes. You can try out other fonts though, but be sure that it is a font that will be on other computers so that people you send it to via email can open and read it at their end.

Font size 11 is highly recommended and size 12 can be appropriate as a minimum. Font sizes higher than 12 can also stress the eyes so do not be tempted to increase your font size to cover up for a scanty CV.

Be consistent and ensure you stick to one font throughout your CV. Having different fonts can be uneasy on the eyes. Note that your name and Headings can carry a bigger bolder typeface.

Margins and Line Spacing: it is best to use the normal margins and line spacing that comes by default in MS Word, but sometimes you need more space to keep your CV under two pages. If you do, I will recommend reducing the margins on the page to not less than 0.75 inches on all sides. Whatever you do, ensure your CV is easy on the eyes and easy to read.

A line spacing of 1 is also appropriate throughout your CV but you can also reduce this to create more space especially on the blank lines where you break into a new line. However, ensure that you edit your CV such that the line spacing is also consistent across the sections.

Page Numbers: It will be helpful to add page numbers to your CV to ensure that it does not get missed up with the pile especially if your employer needs to make photocopies of them. I also personally add my name and contact as a footer on each page in a way that it doesn't look distracting. I do this by reducing the gradient of the font colour to about 50-70% black. However, it is not advisable to use headers or footers when submitting your CV to an online Applicant Tracking System. More about this can be found in chapter 4)

Length: Typically, a CV should be two pages of A4 and this would apply for a graduate with only a few years of work experience. But as one progresses in a career to about 4 – 5 years of progressive work experience, it will be okay to have more than two pages of a CV.

Photos, Images and Graphics: Except you are applying for a job in the design and creative industry, you do not need to add any of these. And if you will for a creative industry, be moderate and don't overdo it.

See CV templates in Appendix 1

Finally to wrap up the CV architecture section, Always think about the relevance of everything on your CV. If it is not directly relevant, think hard of how to make it appear relevant. Sometimes you need to think laterally and outside the box. If there is no way to make some experience relevant, leave it out of your CV.

In the next chapter, you will learn exactly how to craft a Winning 'dynamic' CV for every job application you want to apply for.

CHAPTER THREE

THE WINNING CV DYNAMICS

What is a Dynamic CV

By now, you know it will be important to revisit and brush up your CV when you are applying to a new job. Applying the right dynamics during this process will result in what I call a 'Dynamic CV'. A Dynamic CV is more or less a more competitive version of your standard CV for a specific job application.

A dynamic CV is important because you cannot apply to all jobs with the same CV content. In actual fact for best results in your job applications, you should not apply to two different jobs with the same CV.

Now, I will like you to pay close attention as I am about to share a very vital element of what makes a winning CV.

You can't lie about your past work experience as much as you shouldn't fabricate false claims. However, in the present millennium and with the fierce competition for the few available job openings, you will need to be dynamic with how you communicate your job experience and skills which you acquired while working for your past employers to the new employer

To drive home my point, take a look at the scenario below

Ben worked with company XYZ as an Administrative Officer and his job description as is on his employment letter is as seen in 'sample D' below

KEY RESPONSIBILITIES
- Execute administrative duties and office procedures such as word processing and responding to emails.
- Respond to customer enquiries either face to face or on the phone maintaining professional and effective client contact, counselling, follow-up and feedback
- Assist in organizing and coordinating meetings and trainings
- Recording minutes of meetings.
- Writing and editing materials to be used in brand communication in letters, fliers, brochures, email or website.
- Manage social media engagement for effective brand communication and to increase client base.
- Performs other duties or special projects as required from time to time.

Sample D.

However, on the Job, Ben's major routine was, sorting files and managing the file storage, recording minutes of team meetings, collating all departmental reports and submitting them to the manager, performing various other functions which actually includes running some 'errands' for the Admin Manager and one occasion, he represented her at a meeting she was running late for because he was the one who compiled the report and designed the power point presentation.

On another occasion, Ben actually travelled with the company field staffs who were handling a special SOAR project for one of their new clients and the Admin manager asked him to go with the team so he could handle all the paper work, typing of

The Winning CV Blueprint

reports, running prints and photocopies on the field so they could beat the deadline.

That meant, he also had to attend the technical meetings with the clients and he proved really useful as a member of the field team who were extremely glad that they had an extra hand to help with some of the tasks.

Ben worked at XYZ for two years and was ready to move on so he updated his CV with the job description that was on his appointment as seen in 'Sample D'.

Ben saw another advert for a new job at company ABC and having gone through the job roles, he believes he will excel on the new job although company ABC is recruiting for a Project Officer and listed the following job requirements in Sample E for this role.

Project Support Officer
Key Requirements:
- Experience supporting field projects both on the field and from the office.
- Experience directly supporting Project Managers on day to day project activities
- Manage the project database and provide such information to monitor and track timelines
- Ability to engage high level stakeholders and disseminate information through presentations and briefings.
- Ability to build a good working relationship with partners to drive performance and delivery.
- Experience managing training, meeting and event logistics
- Strong communication skills both written and oral.
- Ability to use Microsoft office, projects and Outlook

Sample E

The Winning CV Blueprint

If Ben goes ahead to submit his CV containing the job description in D, chances are that he will not get any feedback from the employer. Put yourself in the employer's shoes, you want to recruit someone to do 'E' but does it look like the person described in 'D' can perform those tasks?

If Ben were to write a winning CV, he will need to write another dynamic version of his current CV.

How does Ben do this? Let us look at a step by step process.

Steps to Write a Dynamic CV
Step 1: Read the job advert carefully to understand the job roles.

Job roles are the actual tasks to be done on the job. Since job titles vary and mean different things in various firms. i.e. Business Development Officer in one firm might be referred to as Clients Relationship Officer in another firm although they perform exactly the same roles. This is why it is important to read the job role or responsibilities as it clearly states the actual task to be carried out on the job. No matter what they call the job title, if the tasks are things you can do. Then you can proceed, if it is a task you do not have the experience or skill to handle, then do not bother to proceed with the application.

Step 2: Read the job advert carefully to understand the key requirements for the job.

The Winning CV Blueprint

The key requirement specifies the minimum requirements the candidate must have to fit into the role. This varies across companies and will include educational level, years of experience, certification and certain skills and technical abilities.

Some adverts go on to identify the requirements that are 'must haves' and those that are desirable. This means that the skills labeled as Desirable are negotiable and you can still apply if you do not have them at all. In all, gauge the requirements to know if you have what they require and see if you can demonstrate in writing that you have most of what they require.

Step 3: Note down the most important points identified in step 1 and 2 above. Note the keywords and phrases used in the job advert. Sometimes, everything listed is important so go ahead to make notes directly on a PC or on your notepad, whichever works for you.

Step 4: Match the skills and experiences on your current CV with skill and experiences for the new job. Begin to make draw parallels and similarities on the skills and requirements that you have identified that you meet easily.

Reflect on your other work experiences including volunteering, informal work and life experiences and see if you can draw up any transferrable skills and experiences that will match the requirement for the new job you are applying for. This is the defining point where you begin to see for yourself whether you have a great chance at the job or you don't.

Step 5: Refine your new CV by mirroring the language used in the job advert on your new your CV. Use the exact keywords and phrases on the job advert in you CV where ever possible.

For each work experience on your CV, you are free to rearrange the roles and responsibilities so that the areas where you have the strongest match to the new job comes first

Now that you have seen the 5 steps, you will need to practice again and again to master the art of doing this effortlessly. Follow these 5 steps without lying about your past job roles or experiences and you would be putting your best foot forward, blowing your trumpet to harmonize with the music of the employer.

Let's get back to Ben, who has now seen these five steps and has applied them to apply for the job role now has a dynamic version of his CV as seen in 'Sample F'.

Take a good look at F. Does it look like the kind of Person CompanyABC wants to recruit as a Project Support Officer? Absolutely Yes!Although Ben does not meet all the requirements ordinarily, he has been able to demonstrate on his dynamic CV that he has what ABC need without providing false information.

Ben has not provided false information because he has proof for everything he wrote on the dynamic CV. If he is invited for an interview, he can back it all up with verifiable information.

Administrative Officer, Company XYZ
Key Responsibilities

- Supported projects from the office and on the field
- Providing administrative support to Managerial level staff on a day to day basis
- Representing Manager in meeting and high level stakeholder engagement
- Coordinating meetings and training and handling logistics
- Writing and editing of materials for brand communication in letters, brochures and on the website

Sample F

Be like Ben.

Practice these 5 steps every time you want to apply for a new job and you will have in your hands a Winning CV that will catch the attention of any employer any day, anytime.

While there isn't space to talk about cover letters in this book, if you apply these same principles of writing dynamic CVs in writing a cover letter, you would have increased the chances of getting your CV shortlisted for an interview invitation.

CHAPTER FOUR

FINE POINTS OF THE WINNING CV

Types of CVs
When it comes to CVs that gets the attention of employers there are two kinds of CVs largely determined by the emphasis being on either the work history or the skills.

The first is Chronological CV and the Second is a Skills based or Functional CV.

A Chronological CV is the standard CV and the most common type which I have also described in chapter 2 of this book. It focuses on your work history starting with the most recent job you have had and it is easy for employers to follow your work history.

It works well for job seeker with good, solid and relevant work experience.

See *Appendix 1* for an example of a standard CV. Download the template through this link Access Free CV Templates

A Skills based CV is one which focuses on your skills and rather than a chronological list of your Work Experience. This kind of CV will readily demonstrate that you have the skills required to succeed on the new job. On a skills based CV, you might list your workhistory briefly at the later end of the CV or you might not include the work experience section at all. However, it is preferable you include a work experience section as it then achieves a sort of hybrid between a Chronological and Functional CV and employers get a better picture of the candidate in question.

Skills based CV works well for fresh graduates with little or no significant work experience, for those who are changing careers and for those who have huge gaps in their employment history.

See *Appendix 2* for an example of a skill based CV. Download the template through this link Access Free CV Templates

Writing CVs in Difficult Situations:
There are some situations when it really becomes difficult to write a CV that will be competitive. Such situations include being a recent graduate with little no work experience, changing careers, getting a full time role with previous part time work experience and so on. However, there are ways around this to still put in a strong application despite the seeming disadvantages. Let's take a look at a few of them.

Recent Graduate with Little or No Experience
Coursework: If you are a fresh graduate with little or no work experience, you can give your CV more value by highlighting the relevant modules you covered during the course that could prove useful on the job you are applying for. You can also include any significant projects and research work carried out. However, ensure you keep it short, succinct and very relevant.

The Winning CV Blueprint

Work Experience: Write out the few work experience that you have had especially if it is very relevant to the role. If it is not, you might want to consider using a skill-based CV which would present your skills in a better perspective.

To write a skill based CV effectively, list out the skills required for the job you are applying to and for each of them identify where and how you have developed the skill in the past. Go ahead to aggregate all of the experiences under each skill. Then do the same for the other skill requirements.

Here, your formal job roles, Informal role, leadership roles, volunteering roles and other similar experiences all count. You will need to be very creative to draw from you many formal and informal experiences.

In addition, if you have had a lot of small jobs that might make your CV look scanty, it may be better to congregate all the small jobs under one heading i.e. lots of short-term assistant role can be congregated under the heading 'Various Customer Service Jobs.

Changing Careers

When changing careers, it might also be a big hurdle to convince the new employer of your motive for changing and the secondly being able to demonstrate that you can fit into the new career and role without falling short of your responsibilities.

You can demonstrate your passion for the new career obviously by showing that you have taken some relevant trainings to introduce you or entrench you into the new career.

You can also demonstrate your passion by talking about other positive aspects. Write in a way that shows you are genuinely interested in the job and how you have been keeping up to date with the development in the industry, following the trends and attending events.

Dealing With Gaps in Your Career

There could be many reasons why you have gaps in your employment history. Maybe you took out time to go to school or raise a family, or you were made redundant, or you travelled to a new place to settle.

If the gaps are short and less than 12 months in between your work experiences, you can tone down the gaps by only specifying the years in your employment history and not months.

So for example if you had a gap between June 2012 and November 2013 and between Feb 2015 and November 2015, you can write your CV without showing the months as seen below.

- Project Support Officer, Company ABC   2015 – 2016
- Administrative Officer, XYZ Enterprises   2013 – 2015
- Administrative Assistant, Company ACE   2010 - 2012

If you cannot tone down the gaps especially if they are recent, then you will need to provide an explanation for the gap in your cover letter. If it is a gap very much in the past, you should not focus your effort trying to explain why, rather focus on the years where you have had no gap in employment.

The Winning CV Blueprint

Where you need to provide an explanation, be positive about the experience and mention how you continued to develop your skills during the period. If it was a tough period, explain how you overcame the obstacles and what you have learnt in the process. Be careful not to provide false information which can jeopardize your application altogether.

See some examples of positive explanations for employment gaps.

- *I spent the time developing my workplace skills by attending Career Seminars and Skills training.*

- *While searching for jobs that fitted my career objectives, I was developing my skills in writing applications and practicing for interviews skills and I also........*

- *During that time, I completed a part-time basic computing course and developed technical skills for ....*

- *In the period, I volunteered my time at a local NGO where I performed ....*

Getting Your Winning CV to Recruiters

Saving your CV
File Name: Sometimes, the job advert will specify the way you should name your CV. If they do, ensure you follow the instruction to the letter. If however, they did not specify, as a standard, always save your CV with your first name and last

name and then maybe another identifier such as the job role, location, company name and so on. For example;

> *Love Peace CV_Admin Officer 2018.docx*
> *Ben Joy CV_Ogun_Company ABC.pdf*

This is important because recruiters get a lot of CVs for various roles they are recruiting for. It is therefore very easy for your CV to get lost in the pile if they cannot seem to trace your CV to the role you are applying for

Format: The most important information here is to follow the application instructions for the job in case they have specified the number of pages and format you should send your CV in be it MS word or PDF.

PDFs are safer when sending documents that are format sensitive to another person because a PDF format ensures the format stays intact when downloaded at the other end.

Recent MS Word version come with an option to save your work as a PDF file and if not, you can visit www.smallpdf.com to convert your CV from word to PDF version.

Emailing your Application

Email Subject: Recruiters sometimes specify what the subject of the email should be, you must adhere to this instruction if you want your application to be received and read. The recruiter's email settings could have been set up to put all emails with that exact subject in a dedicated folder and if anyone does not comply, that email by default will not get into the pool of applications that would be considered.

The Winning CV Blueprint

Email Body: Some people have the habit of leaving the email body blank when applying for a job. Amidst the strong competition, this is a great disadvantage. Never send your application without writing a body for your email.

What you will write doesn't have to be long and it could be as little as two lines. But it is a fantastic opportunity to get the attention of the recruiter from the very time your email is opened. Do a brief introduction and communicate your expertise and interest in the role. Do this as briefly as possible as you are already sending a cover letter which will do most of the talking with your CV.

You should always do this whether a Cover Letter is requested for or not because it stands you out automatically. You can keep your email body to a maximum of 5 lines.

Likewise, you should always compose a new email for every job application. No matter the excuse of access to internet or lack of a computer to work with, never forward a previous email from your inbox or sent items with your CV attached to another employer. It is so unprofessional and it will not speak well of you.

As a sample email body, you can write

> *Dear HR,*
>
> *Please find attached my cover letter and CV for your perusal in response to the open position for an Administrative Assistant in Benue State. I have the required skills and experience to succeed on this job and I look forward to joining the team at XYZ Enterprises.*

Yours Faithfully,
Love Joy.

Understanding Applicant Tracking Systems

By now, you should know that large organizations especially multinationals use an online recruitment system to screen the thousands of applications they receive. This system is called the Applicant Tracking System (ATS).

The system works by quickly scanning the database of submitted CVs matching them with the criteria of the job being applied for. It scans for key words and specific phrases that the employer has specified in the job description and person specification. CVs that do not meet up a certain matching score would not see the light of the day and would never be seen or read by a human.

Only CVs that meets up to a certain score are forwarded to the employer so a human can then review the CVs and further shortlist the potential candidates.

However, you can use the software to your advantage. The keywords and phrases used to search the application database will include job titles, job roles, key skills, required certifications and professional memberships.

To use the ATS to your advantage, revise the 5 steps explained in chapter three of this book paying particular attention to steps 4 and 5 and then note the following points.

- Provide the full titles and acronyms of your qualifications or the names of organizations you have worked. For example,

The Chartered Institute of Management (CIM) - Certificate in Project Management, June 2013 – July 2015

- Dates should appear at the end of your qualification or work experience rather than at the start. Dates at the beginning can confuse the ATS in its search for keywords. This example is used in the previous point above.

- Use standard fonts such as Arial, Calibri, Georgia, Tahoma or Verdana.

- Leave out special characters and avoid non-standard bullet styles.

- Do not use headers and footers, tables, graphics and logos.

- Except otherwise stated, submit your CV as a word document (.doc), text (.txt) or rich text (.rtf) file. Only submit a PDF to an online platform except you are instructed to do so or you are sure a human will read it and not the system.

APPENDICES

(To get a soft copy of various CV templates, visit the link below Access Free CV Templates and click on 'Get Started')

Appendix 1–Standard CV Sample

LOVE PEACE

10 Goke Adrion Street, Kano Estate, Kano
Mob: +234 7679632572 | love.peace@yahoo.com

PERSONAL OBJECTIVE

I aspire to rise to the peak of my career as a _____ by continually challenging myself and evolving in my leadership and organization skills to build a world class identity within the _____ industry.

EDUCATION & QUALIFICATIONS

2014	**Foundationin Travel and Tourism (Diploma)** International Air Transport Association (IATA)
2007 - 2012	**B.Tech in Transport Management** Federal University of Technology, Akure, Ondo State.
2000 - 2006	**West African Secondary School Certificate Examination** Oaisis Model College, ibadan, Oyo State.

PAID WORK EXPERIENCE

Feb 2016 – Jun 2016   **Reservation Officer, Dolphin Travels and Tours, Lagos.**
Responsibilities:
- Performed general office and administrative functions including managing office supplies
- Was responsible for handling reservations for clients
- Increased company customer base for the flight booking and tourism packages.

Jan 2015 – Dec 2015   **Customer Care Officer, Nusra Travels and Tours, Abuja.**
Responsibilities:
- Handled reservations for clients
- Followed up on customer service requests and enquiries.
- Managed company aviation accounts including BSP reconciliations and other financial record books

Aug 2011 - Jan 2012   **Aviation Duty Officer, FAAN, Muritala Local Airport, Lagos**
Responsibilities:
- Carried out routine Inspection and maintenance checks of the airside (i.e. apron), landside (i.e.

car park) and terminals (i.e. rest rooms, lounges.).
- Responsible for notifying units and departmental heads of any faults or maintenance issues including mechanical, electrical, water and sewage problems in the airport.
- Monitored such repairs till they are completed and rectified.

VOLUNTARY EXPERIENCE & PROJECTS

Mar 2013–Feb 2014 **Volunteer,** Tourism Community Development Service
As a volunteer, I worked with a team that established travel and tourism club in eight secondary schools within Lokoja engaging about 1000 students altogether.

Nov 2012 - date **Volunteer, Feed Nigeria**
Participated in organizing 'eat and cook sessions' using unwanted food gathered from stores to feed people within deprived communities.

Jun 2011 - Sept 2013 **Coordinator, Redeemed Christian Fellowship**
Was responsible for coordination of a 3-weeks summer school programme for indigent secondary school students and supervising other volunteers. Also taught computer studies and biology to the participants.

PROFESSIONAL DEVELOPMENT

       Conferences & Seminars
June 2014 Water and Food sustainability conference and award, London
April 2014 The Science of Bones, Life seminar series, University of Sheffield

LEADERSHIP ROLES

2013 - 2014 **General Secretary**, Tourism Community Development Service

HONOURS & AWARDS

Dec. 2014 Excellence Award, Sheffield Hallam Nigerian Society
July 2014 Sheffield Business School Leadership Award

RESEARCH & PUBLICATIONS

Ogidan G. (2012) *Analysis of Passenger's Air Traffic in Nigeria*. Unpublished *Bachelor Thesis*.

SKILLS

- Ability to adapt quickly to change and new environments.
- A resourceful team player with excellent Organizational, Communication, and Leadership skills.
- Ability to 'get on' with people from different social and cultural backgrounds.

COMPUTER & IT SKILLS

- Good working knowledge of Sabre and Amadeus global distribution system.
- Proficient use of Microsoft packages (Word, Excel, and PowerPoint)

LANGUAGES

English (Fluent), Yoruba (Fluent)

HOBBIES

Travelling to historic locations and reading auto-biographies.

The Winning CV Blueprint

Appendix 2-Skill Based CV Sample
LOVE JOY
1 Career Road, Career Town, Career County XX1 4BE
Tel: 01234 555 666 (Home) / 07951 123 456 (Mobile)
Email: susanbarker@career.co.uk

PROFESSIONAL PROFILE
A multi-skilled, part-qualified HR professional with excellent all-round HR advisory skills and experience. Proven leadership skills, including managing and motivating others to achieve company objectives. Possesses exceptional interpersonal and relationship management skills. Experienced in providing timely and up-to-date HR advice to both managers and employees. Extensive knowledge of working practices, recruitment and retention, compensation and benefits and training and development. Currently studying towards full CIPD status. Now seeking next challenging role with a blue chip company.

SKILLS AND EXPERIENCE
Reward Management
- Implemented company incentive schemes which have reduced absenteeism and increased production levels by 15% at A&B Insurance
- Increased participation and managed the company's share ownership scheme
- Facilitated regular reviews and benchmarking of salaries to ensure compensation is consistent within industry sectors

Human Resource Planning
- Assessed companies' future staffing requirements over the short, medium and long-term and made recommendations concerning re-organisations to senior management
- Produced a comprehensive Human Resources plan for the company's expansion over the next five years whilst at C&D Insurance

Employee Relations
- Extensive handling of managing redundancies and displacements
- Re-wrote policies on gross misconduct, disciplinaries and grievance procedures supported and coached managers in the resolution of ER issues
- Offered advisory service on all aspects of employee performance management and development

Recruitment & Selection
- Conducted competency-based interviews for candidates across all levels including senior positions
- Re-wrote job specifications and designed job adverts utilising most cost-effective method of advertising
- Supervised HR Assistant in co-ordinating job interviews and conducting pre-employment checks
- Made recommendations to hiring managers regarding candidate selection

Process and Procedure
- Supervised HR teams in managing and maintaining accurate and up-to-date staff personnel records
- Attendance at employment law updates and advised senior HR staff on policy and procedure changes

Training and Development
- Designed and delivered Induction programmes for new employees
- Appointed and monitored external training organisations for specialist training courses

- Implemented company-wide training needs analysis and advised on most productive learning methods
- Managed a training budget and produced reports for senior management
- Led 'lunchtime learning' opportunities for managers in 'Understanding Policies' and how they should be implemented for managing their teams

CAREER SUMMARY

2011 - 2012	A&B INSURANCE, Staines, *HR Officer*
2008 - 2009	C&D INSURANCE, Staines *HR Advisor (contract)*
2007 - 2008	E&F INSURANCE, Staines, *HR Advisor (contract)*
2003 - 2006	G&H INSURANCE, Staines, *HR Assistant*
2000 - 2003	I&J INSURANCE, Staines, *Office Manager*
1998 - 2000	K&L INSURANCE, Staines, *Receptionist*

EDUCATION AND TRAINING

Intermediate Diploma in Human Resource Management (CIPD), HR College, Staines, 2011
Certificate in Personnel Practice (CIPD), HR College, Staines, 2008
BTEC in Business Studies, Staines, 1998
8 GCSEs (including English & Maths), Staines, 1996

FURTHER COURSES

Managing Teams, 2010
Performance Management for HR Professionals, 2009
Coaching and Feedback for HR Professionals, 2009
Communication Skills in the Workplace, 2008
Time Management and Organisational Skills, 2008
Advanced Excel, 2008

PROFESSIONAL MEMBERSHIPS

Associate: Chartered Institute of Personnel and Development (CIPD)

ADDITIONAL INFORMATION

IT Skills: Advanced Word, Excel and Powerpoint
Languages: Intermediate Spanish
Qualified First Aider

INTERESTS

Swimming, member of local badminton club, playing piano, cooking Thai & Indian Food

REFERENCES ARE AVAILABLE ON REQUEST

Appendix 3–Career Specific CV Types

Technical CV
This is a kind of CV mostly needed for IT and very technical roles. It should highlight in details the specific technical skills you have that are related to the role (eg programming languages, systems, platforms) alongside the all-important 'softer skills' that all employers are looking for.

Creative industries CV
CV formats for the creative industry can be creative and imaginative to reflect ingenuity. A highly creative CV format can help you stand out from the crowd especially in the creative and artistic sectors i.e design, journalism or advertising. Infographics can be used and your portfolio can be presented in a creative way. You can put your portfolio on a website and include the web address in your CV. If you do this, make sure your work is structured and indexed, well photographed and highlights the range of your work which is relevant to the role.

Video CV
Video CVs are becoming more popular in recent times and in a few years, it will be more popular and might come to be a generally acceptable method of submitting CVs. Video CVs are currently more popular in customer-facing and creative roles as it gets the recruiter to see the personality of the applicants first hand. A good video CV will emphasize on the contents, confidence and ability to communicate what you have to offer in a clear and succinct, yet convincing way.

Academic CV

To apply for research or lecturing positions in the academia, you will require an academic CV. Academic CVs are different and can contain other sections and include a detailed list of Research Work & Interests, Funding received, Seminar Papers and Presentations, Books and Publications, Conferences attended Memberships, and so on. It will also highlight the teaching experience and leadership position.

About the Book

In this book, you will learn

- How to write a job landing CV from scratch.
- How to think like the employer and write a CV that stands out
- How to communicate your skills and experience so that employers can shortlist you for an interview.
- How to edit your CV for every job you are applying for in a way that presents you as the best candidate.
- How to handle job applications and use it to your advantage if you have limited job experience, are changing career or have employment gap
- And so much more.

The Winning CV Blueprint is a hands-on practical guide to teach students, recent graduates and young professionals how to sell themselves as an ideal candidate for any job.

This book was written from an expert point of view, haven had a first-hand experience of applying and interviewing for 5 good jobs within a space of 5years across two continents and having helped countless number of people review their CVs and applications to get a job or win a competition.

About the Author

Ebenezer is a health, life and business coach with expertise in professional and business writing helping start-ups, professionals and businesses build their personal and corporate brands by communicating effectively in writing whether for content development, application letters, business plans and proposals of various kinds.

As a public health specialist, he works to promote positive behaviour change for the prevention and control of non-communicable diseases through his social enterprise- Healthucate Limited.

He is also passionate about addressing teenage audiences on issues around purpose discovery and relationships and he is the author of the book 'Handling the Teenage Years' – a life resource for teenagers and those who care for them.

Ebenezer is an alumnus of the Sheffield Business School in the United Kingdom, a Tony Elumelu Entrepreneur, Common Purpose 360° leader, Ashoka Changemaker fellow, an alumnus of Junior Achievement Nigeria and LEAP Africa.

He is married to his best friend and is a father to an amazing young lad. He enjoys playing the piano and appreciates every form of art.

CONNECT WITH ME

WEBSITE	www.iamebenezer.com
LINKEDIN	Linkedin.com/in/ebenezer.anifowose
TWITTER	Twitter.com/opeldexter
FACEBOOK	Facebook.com/eanifowose
INSTAGRAM	Intagram.com/opeldexter

Join the Learn To Write Community on facebook to connect and interact with other people like you who are learning to write positively and competitively. Join to get support to crush your career, life and business goals.

WWW.FACEBOOK.COM/GROUPS/LEARN2WRITE

www.ingramcontent.com/pod-product-compliance
Lightning Source LLC
Chambersburg PA
CBHW031548210526
45464CB00003B/1202